The almost instant assembly book

12 complete acts of
worship for primary schools

Sue & Chris Govus

Kevin
Mayhew

First published in 1999 by
KEVIN MAYHEW LTD
Buxhall
Stowmarket
Suffolk IP14 3BW

4 5 6 7 8 9

ISBN 1 84003 373 8
Catalogue No 1500273

Cover design by Jonathan Stroulger
Illustrations by Stephen Greenfield
Edited by Elisabeth Bates
Typesetting by Richard Weaver
Printed in Great Britain

Contents

Introduction _____

Having worked in schools taking RE lessons and assemblies (acts of worship) for the last nine years, we have been encouraged by many teachers to put some of our ideas down on paper. We are very aware of the many pressures put on teaching staff today and for them to find preparation time for an 'assembly' is not always top priority! With this in mind, we have tried to produce a book of 'almost instant' acts of worship that may be of some help.

We have attempted to write the book so that, if necessary, each 'assembly' could be read as written. However, our desire is that using the structure provided, teachers will feel able and confident to inject their own character and personality into the telling of these stories.

The illustrations and cue words in this book can be reproduced by photocopying them onto acetate film designed to be used with photocopiers. They can then be used black and white or you may decide to add some colour by use of OHP pens.

You may prefer to photocopy them onto A4 paper or enlarge them to A3 size. They can then be coloured with paints/pencils or even given to children in your class to prepare them for you before hand! Pictures can also be used as a classroom frieze.

We sincerely hope that this book will assist you in the preparation and presentation of assemblies so that you and the children will enjoy and learn from your 'acts of worship'.

Sue and Chris Govus
Back 2 School Ministries
September 1998

CREATION _____

Bible Reference   Genesis 1 and 2

Aim
- To think about our world.
- Is it important to us?
- How can we enjoy it and look after it?

Introduction   We live in an amazing universe on a wonderful planet. Scientists tell us it's in just the right place in the solar system. Any closer to our sun and we would fry, any further away and we would freeze!

Christians don't believe that life on this planet came about by accident or chance but by design.

Lots of people have different ideas as to how the universe began and as you get older you'll hear lots of different viewpoints and need to decide for yourself what you choose to believe. Today we are going to hear what the Bible says about the creation of the universe.

Bible Story   The Bible tells us that no one created God, he was always there. It also tells us that it was God who created the universe and everything in it. In the very beginning the earth was empty, covered in water and darkness was everywhere. When God spoke things happened! On the very first day of creation . . .

Picture 1   God said 'Let there be light,' and there was light. God then separated the light from the darkness and called the light – DAY and the darkness he called NIGHT.

God looked at what he had made and saw that . . .

Picture 8   IT WAS GOOD – *(You might like to encourage the children to read these words out loud)*

Picture 2   On the second day God separated the water and he made the sea and the sky.

Then God looked at what he had created and saw that . . .

Picture 8   IT WAS GOOD

Picture 3   On the third day God gathered the sea-water together and created dry ground which he called land. At God's command vegetation began to grow on the land, every variety of grass, plants, trees and flowers.

God looked at what he had made and saw that . . .

Picture 8   IT WAS GOOD

Picture 4   On the fourth day God created all the things we see in the sky and beyond, the sun, moon, stars and planets.

God looked at what he had made and saw that . . .

Picture 8   IT WAS GOOD

Picture 5   On the fifth day God created all the creatures that live in the sea, every variety of fish and shellfish, whales, dolphins. He also created all the birds that fly in the sky and the ones that can't fly.

God looked at all he had made and saw that . . .

Picture 8   IT WAS GOOD

Picture 6   On the sixth day God created all the creatures that live on dry land; elephants, pandas, lions, even the creepy crawly ants and spiders. Finally God created a man and a woman. Adam and Eve. He made them very special and different from all the other creatures. He gave them the very important job of looking after all the animals and taking care of the earth.

God looked at what he had created and saw that . . .

Picture 8   IT WAS VERY GOOD

Picture 7   On the seventh day God rested. God had created a beautiful universe for us to explore and enjoy, he knew . . .

Picture 8   IT WAS VERY GOOD

Application

God created a wonderful world and Adam, as the first man, was given the responsibility of caring for it. Everything Adam needed to live on the earth was provided for him: water, food, air to breathe. Today, these things are still provided for us, but are we caring for our world in the way that we should?

- Are we using the water we have wisely? *(If hosepipe bans are in place you may want to discuss this further.)*

- Do we share the food we have around the world fairly so everyone has enough to eat?

- Is our air still good to breathe or are we polluting it by the things we put into it?

- Are we caring for the wildlife or destroying it with our pollution and litter?

We may not be able to look after the whole world, but we can look after the area we live in, around our homes, our school – think about what you can do to look after your world and make it a better place to live.

Suggested Songs

All things bright and beautiful (*Junior Praise, 6; Kidsource, 8*)

He's got the whole wide world (*Junior Praise, 78*)

My God is so big (*Junior Praise, 169; Kidsource, 255*)

Who put the colours in the rainbow? (*Junior Praise, 288; Kidsource, 386*)

Closing Thoughts/Prayer

Dear God,

thank you for giving us such a lovely world in which to live.

Please help us to think about our actions.

Show us how to look after our world and how we can make it a better place for others to live in.

Amen.

Possible Classroom Follow-up

- Discuss
  - Who and what pollutes our world?
  - How can we help to prevent it being damaged or destroyed?
  - What can we do to protect the wildlife we see around us?
- Make a collage of the Creation story.
- Consider a CDT project to help wildlife, e.g. make a birdbox or birdtable.

IT WAS
GOOD

IT WAS
VERY
GOOD

Picture 8

DAVID AND GOLIATH _____

Bible Reference   1 Samuel 17

Aim   To think how we react when facing difficulties, such as bullying:

- do we try to run away?

- do we carry on and pretend it's not happening? *or,*

- do we face up to the problem and deal with it?

Introduction   Do you have a hero? Someone you look up to and admire. *(You may want to take feedback from the children.)* Many books are full of heroes and heroines and the Bible is no exception. In our story today we are going to hear about two armies who met to do battle. Each army had someone in it whom the people regarded as their hero. However, the real hero of this story was neither of them.

Bible Story   *(This story has been written for audience participation – as the appropriate sound effect is shown the children are encouraged to respond. You may find it helpful to have one person narrating the story and another responsible for displaying the cue words.)*

Saul was king of Israel and in charge of the Israelite army. He had helped his army win many battles and for the Israelite people, Saul was the greatest **(Hooray)**. One day Saul heard that the Philistines were preparing to do battle with Israel **(Oh No!)**. So Saul got his army together and marched them out to meet the Philistines. They met in the Valley of Elah. The Israelites with their great leader Saul on one hill **(Hooray)** and the Philistines glaring at them from across the valley on another hill **(Boo)**.

The hero of the Philistine army was called Goliath **(Boo)**. He was a really big guy and stood about 3 metres tall **(Wow!)**. He marched out of the Philistine camp and shouted across the valley to the Israelite army, 'Choose a man to come and fight me, if he can kill me, then these Philistines will be your slaves **(Wow!)** but if I can kill him, then you must all become our slaves' **(Oh No!)**. The Israelite army was terrified, even King Saul decided he was not going to face Goliath **(No Way)**.

Goliath continued with his challenge every morning and evening for the next forty days. The Israelites were desperate – who would go and fight Goliath? King Saul tried to encourage one of his men to go by offering a large sum of money **(No Way)**, he tried bribing them with no more tax bills **(No Way)**, he even said they could marry his daughter **(No Way)**. No one was brave enough to go and fight Goliath! **(Oh No!)**.

Meanwhile, back in Bethlehem, a young shepherd boy called David was out in the fields looking after his father's sheep **(Baa)**. Three of David's older brothers were in Saul's army and so his father asked him to take some food supplies to them. He also wanted news from the battlefield. David left the sheep with another shepherd **(Baa)** and set off towards the Valley of Elah.

When he arrived, he left the food he had been carrying at the supplies depot and ran to find his brothers. While he was talking to them, Goliath appeared across the valley **(Oh No!)** and shouted out his challenge. 'Choose a man to come and fight me, if he can kill me, then these Philistines will be your slaves, but if I can kill him, then you must all become our slaves.' **(Gulp)**.

David got very angry, because Goliath was taking the mickey out of the Israelites and their God and everyone was scared to fight him. David knew that God was on their side, **(Hooray)** so he said bravely, 'With God's help, I'll take care of that Philistine' **(Wow!)**.

His eldest brother said to him, **(No Way)** 'Don't be so stupid, go back to Bethlehem and look after the sheep' **(Baa)**.

But King Saul got to hear what David was saying and summoned him to his tent. 'Don't worry about a thing,' David told him, 'I know God is with us and I will go and fight Goliath and win' **(Wow)**. King Saul laughed at David, **(Ha Ha)**. 'You're only a boy, Goliath is a trained fighter' **(Gulp)**. But David persisted, he explained to Saul how he had fought lions and bears that were attacking his sheep **(Baa)**, God had protected him then and God would protect him now **(Hooray)**. Finally Saul agreed to let him go and fight, and offered David his armour to wear. However, Saul's armour was much too big and heavy for little David **(Oh No)**. 'I can't wear this,' David said, 'I can hardly move'. He took the armour off and ran down to the stream, picked up five smooth stones which he put in his shepherd's bag, then with his shepherd's staff and sling started across the valley towards Goliath **(Gulp)**.

Goliath saw David coming towards him and laughed **(Ha Ha)**, he shouted abuse at David and took the mickey out of him, but David stood up for himself and replied, 'Today, with God's help I will fight you and win'. Goliath roared with laughter **(Ha Ha)**. David ran closer to him, reaching into his shepherd's bag he took out a stone, put it in his sling and swung it around. The stone left the sling at massive speed and smashed into the middle of Goliath's forehead. The Philistine crashed to the ground like a felled tree **(Wow!)**. Swiftly David ran over to him, then taking Goliath's sword in both hands, he chopped off the Philistine's head **(Gulp)**. The Israelites were absolutely delighted **(Hooray)**. However, on the other side of the valley, the Philistines **(Boo)**, seeing that their hero was now dead were terrified and began to run away **(Hooray)**. The now brave Israelites rushed after them, chasing them out of Israel.

David, just a young shepherd boy, had with God's help, beaten the bully and saved the nation from a humiliating defeat and almost certain slavery – what a hero! **(Hooray)**.

Application

Goliath was a very real bully. It needed someone to stand up to him. Interestingly, the Philistines were only brave while Goliath was around, once he was killed they ran. King Saul did not want to face the giant, he and his army just sat around for days doing nothing, probably hoping the problem would go away. David knew that action had to be taken and did something about it.

Think about your reaction when facing difficulties:

- do you try and run away from them?

- do you do nothing, hoping the problem will disappear? *or*

- do you face up to them and try and sort it out?

Is there a problem that needs sorting today?

Suggested Songs

My God is so big (*Junior Praise*, 169; *Kidsource*, 255)

Only a boy called David (*Junior Praise*, 190)

Closing Thoughts/Prayer

Dear God,

please help us to face up to the difficulties and problems we have and not to run away from them.

Please give us the courage and strength we need to deal with the situation, just like you did for David.

Amen.

Possible Classroom Follow-up

Discuss bullying

- What actions can be taken to deal with this problem?

- What can be done to help: a. the victim; b. the bully?

- What people or agencies are available (in school and elsewhere) to help those with problems and difficulties?

- Is it better to leave a problem alone or face up to it?

Hooray

No Way

Boo

Baa

Wow!

Oh No!

Ha Ha

Gulp

JONAH

Bible Reference   Jonah 1-4

Aim
- To think about the importance of saying sorry when we've made a mistake.

- To realise that if we are genuinely sorry we can have a fresh start.

Introduction   How many of you like having adventures? Today we are going to hear about a man in the Bible who had a really big adventure – but he didn't enjoy it. The truth is, if he had done what he was supposed to do, he would have saved himself a lot of unpleasantness. He made some big mistakes and only when he said sorry did things start to get better.

Bible Story   Our story begins with a man called Jonah, he was known as a prophet, someone who listened to and followed God, until one day . . .

Picture 1   God said to Jonah, 'I want you to go to the City of Nineveh. The people there have stopped listening to me. They are doing cruel and unkind things to each other and unless they change their ways, I'm going to destroy their city. Jonah, I want you to go and warn them.' No way did Jonah want to go to Nineveh. He did not like the people there and couldn't care less if God wanted to destroy them. Jonah decided to run away from God. He went to the harbour at Joppa, found a boat going to Spain (exactly the opposite direction to Nineveh), paid his fare, went on board and fell asleep below the deck.

Picture 2   Jonah woke with a jolt, the captain of the ship was standing by him, 'We're in a really bad storm,' he said to Jonah, 'start praying to your God to save us.'
    Realising what was happening Jonah said, 'The storm's all my fault! The God I serve made the sea, he controls the wind and waves. If you want this storm to stop you'll have to throw me overboard.' The sailors did not want to harm Jonah so they got the oars and tried to row the boat out of danger. However, the storm got worse and worse. Finally, they gave up, picked up Jonah and . . .

Picture 3   . . . threw him overboard! They prayed that God would not hold it against them for killing Jonah. As he plunged into the sea, the storm suddenly stopped. God did not want Jonah to drown, he had other plans for this man. As he was splashing around in the waves a great big fish swam up to him and swallowed him whole.

Picture 4   Once inside the fish's belly, Jonah realised how stupid he had been. He could not run away from God. If only he had gone to Nineveh when God had asked him, he would not be in the mess he now found himself in. He would not have been on a boat, would not have been in a storm and certainly would not now be inside a very smelly fish's tum! Knowing that he had messed up big time, Jonah said sorry to God and three days later the fish vomited him . . .

Picture 5   . . . out onto the beach. Jonah knew he had to do what God wanted, so he set off on his journey to the city of Nineveh. Once he had arrived, he started preaching to the people in the city.

Picture 6   He told them about their cruel, unkind and evil behaviour. He warned them that unless they changed their ways, God would destroy their city. The people listened to and believed Jonah. Even the king of Nineveh realised Jonah was speaking the truth. He called for all the people to repent – that means to say sorry to God. To show that they were sincere they took off their posh clothes, put on old sack cloths and prayed, asking God to forgive them. God knew that the people were genuinely sorry . . .

Picture 7   . . . so he told Jonah that he would no longer destroy their city. Instead of being pleased about this, Jonah got the hump! In a real huff, he went and sat outside the city, under a vine so that he could get some shade from the hot sun. 'I knew God would forgive them,' he thought to himself. 'I wanted him to destroy Nineveh – the people deserved it.'

Picture 8   To teach Jonah something very important, God sent a worm that started eating through the vine and the vine died. Jonah was even more upset, he now had no shade from the sun! It was then that God said to him, 'Jonah, you're annoyed because a plant has died, even though you did nothing to look after it and make it grow. There are over one hundred and twenty thousand people in Nineveh and I love, care and provide for every one of them – surely it's right for me not to destroy them, but to forgive them when they are truly sorry for the evil things they have done.'

Application

Saying sorry is not always easy. However, knowing that we've hurt someone or done something wrong can play on our conscience.

It's much better if we are genuinely sorry to say so, put the mistakes of the past behind us and have a fresh start.

The people of Nineveh recognised they had been doing wrong and were prepared to say sorry and God forgave them. It took Jonah a bit longer to realise his mistake, he kept running from God hoping everything would work out OK. It was only when he got into a real mess that he finally said sorry.

- Is there anyone you need to say sorry to?

- Maybe you need to forgive someone who has hurt you in some way?

- Wouldn't it be good to sort it out and have a fresh start?

Suggested Songs

Come listen to my tale (*Junior Praise*, 30)

Make me a channel of your peace (*Junior Praise*, 161; *Kidsource*, 248)

It's a new day (*Come and Praise*, 106)

Shalom, my friend (*Junior Praise*, 217)

Closing Thoughts/Prayer

Dear God,

please show us how to be honest with ourselves, others and you, by admitting the mistakes we make.

Help us to realise that if we are truly sorry for what we have done, the mistakes we make can be forgiven and we can have a fresh start.

Amen.

Possible Classroom Follow-up

Discuss

- How problems can escalate when we/nations fail to forgive each other (this could then be used to introduce a historical event/topic).

- What are some of the practical ways that we can demonstrate to others that we are genuinely sorry and want their forgiveness?

Picture 1

Picture 2

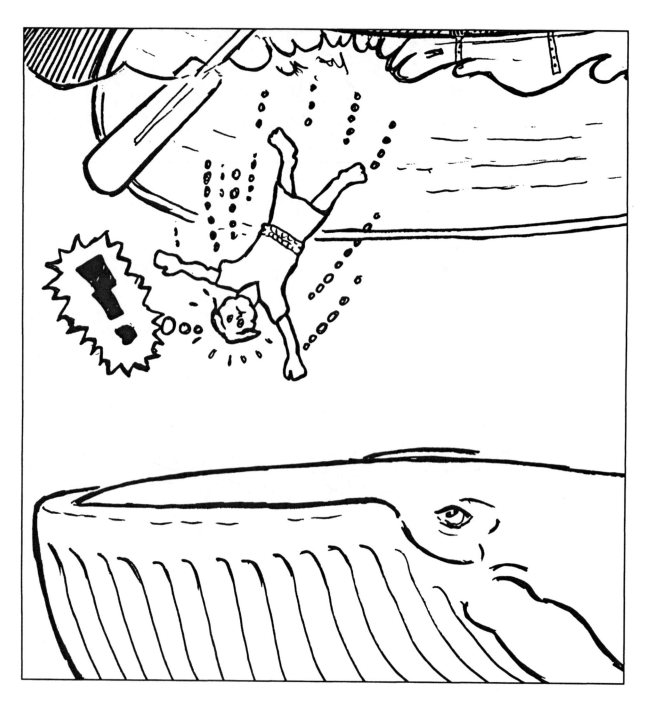

Picture 3

Picture 4

Picture 5

Picture 6

Picture 7

Picture 8

THE BIRTH OF JESUS _____

Bible References   Matthew 1:18-2:18

Luke 2:1-20

Aim   • To see how much the children know about the events surrounding the birth of Jesus.

Introduction   Either: a. Talk from your own experience about Christmas as a child, (possibly cover the excitement or not sleeping Christmas Eve, the eagerness to open presents, family gatherings, that embarrassing present . . .)

or

b. Ask the children what Christmas means to them, what do they think of when you mention the word 'Christmas'? (Turkey, presents, carols, holidays, baby Jesus, decorations, crackers, eating too much, going to church, watching television, etc.) *(You may find it helpful to write their answers down on an OHP or a white/black board.)*

Bible Story   In the New Testament of the Bible we can read about the birth of Jesus. You may know more about the events surrounding his birth than those of any other person in history. Have you ever wondered why that is? Could it be that Jesus really is someone very special?

So let's see, using a crossword quiz, how much you know about his birth. *(You may need to explain a crossword to the children. You can either open the answers up to the first person who puts their hand up or play classes against each other, even boys v girls.)*

12 across   What was the name of Jesus' mother? (MARY)

6 down   An angel visited Mary to tell her she was going to have a ____ (BABY)

22 down   The angel told Mary that this special baby would be God's ____ (SON)

9 across   Mary and Joseph had to go on a journey to what town? ____ (BETHLEHEM)

16 across   It was a long journey, they may have walked or ridden on a ____ (DONKEY)

18 down   They had to go to Bethlehem for a census because it was the ____ (LAW)

6 across   On arrival, Mary and Joseph found the town very ____ (BUSY)

13 across   They needed somewhere to sleep and asked for a room in the ____ (INN)

24 across   What do we call a person who runs an inn? ____ (INNKEEPER)

22 across   All the inns were full, where did they end up sleeping? ____ (STABLE)

19 down   As it was night-time, it was probably very ____ in the stable. (DARK)

11 down   That night Mary's baby was born. Having no cot, she had to ____ him in an animals' feeding trough. (LAY)

2 down   Another name for the animals' feeding trough. (MANGER)

5 down   What name is given to a person who looks after sheep? (SHEPHERD)

8 across   What do we call a female sheep? (EWE)

15 down   Who visited the shepherds to tell them Jesus had been born? (ANGEL)

7 across   The angel spoke to the shepherds saying 'I bring good ____' (NEWS)

4 down   Who else journeyed to visit Jesus? (WISE MEN)

14 down   Which direction did they travel from? (EAST)

20 down   What did they see and decide to follow that led them to Jesus? (STAR)

10 down   What was the name of the King they met with in Jerusalem? (HEROD)

17 across   Herod wanted to know the exact time they ____ the star. (SAW)

13 down   The wise men journeyed to Bethlehem after reading the writings of the prophet Micah. The scroll they read was probably written in ancient ____ (INK)

21 down   One of the three gifts given to Jesus by the wise men ____ (GOLD)

1 across   King Herod really wanted to kill Jesus. The wise men were warned in a ____ not to go back and tell him where Jesus was. (DREAM)

3 & 23 across   All this took place approximately ____ thousand years ago. (TWO)

Application   All this happened about 2,000 years ago, yet today it is still celebrated in many parts of the world because it was such a special event. It's very unlikely that Jesus was actually born on the 25th December, but for various reasons this is the day when Christians choose to celebrate the coming of Jesus.

This Christmas, when you're tucking into your turkey and pulling the crackers, just think for a moment what the real meaning of Christmas is and what is being celebrated – the birth of a special baby.

Suggested Songs

Away in a manger (*Junior Praise*, 12; *Kidsource*, 15)

See him lying on a bed of straw (*Junior Praise*, 214; *Kidsource*, 291)

O little town of Bethlehem (*Junior Praise*, 182)

Closing Thoughts/Prayer

Dear God,

thank you for Christmas time, an opportunity to celebrate the birth of your son.

Please help us all to have a really happy and peaceful Christmas, but not to forget the reason behind the celebrations.

Amen.

Possible Classroom Follow-up

• Make a Nativity scene

• Compare being born in a stable with being born in a maternity hospital.

• Discuss

 – What gifts you would give to a new-born baby?

 – What did the wise men bring?

 – What use were these gifts to a baby?

 – Did these gifts have any special meaning?

GIFT	WHAT IS IT?	A SYMBOL OF
Gold	Precious metallic element	Kingship – to acknowledge Jesus the King.
Frankincense	Aromatic resin from trees (burnt by the priests in worship)	Priesthood – Jesus standing between man and God.
Myrrh	Resin used in perfume and medicine (used to embalm the body)	Death – to show what Jesus had come to do.

CHRISTMAS CROSSWORD

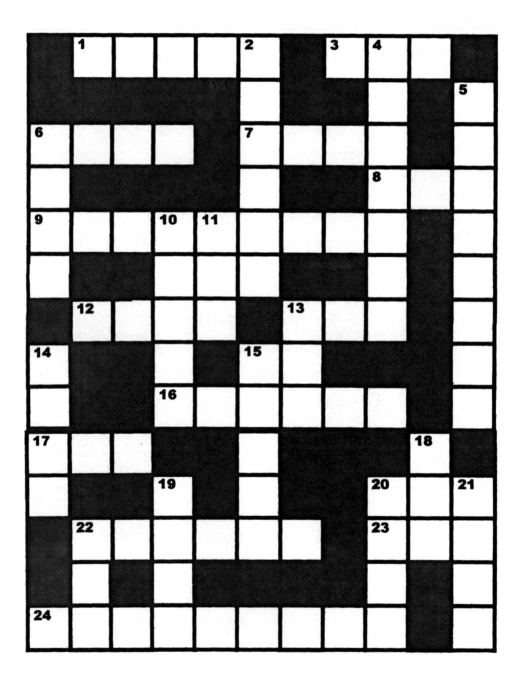

THE FEEDING OF THE 5,000+ _____

Bible References

Matthew 14:13-21

Mark 6:32-44

Luke 9:10-17

John 6:1-13

Aim

To convey to the children that whoever we are, no matter how insignificant we might feel, we all have something worth sharing with others.

Introduction

Who likes to go on a picnic?

Possibly talk about

- Favourite food for picnics

- Best place to have a picnic (beach/countryside/back garden)

- Right weather for a picnic

Today I'm going to tell you a story about one of the most amazing picnics. This picnic was so special that four different people all wrote about it in their books which can be found in the New Testament of the Bible. Their names were Matthew, Mark, Luke and John.

Bible Story

Jesus had done so many amazing things. He was a great teacher and crowds of people would gather around him just to listen to what he had to say. One of the best places for everyone to gather was on the hillside around the Sea of Galilee. (The hills create a natural amphitheatre where no PA equipment is needed – ideal for mass meetings!) On this particular day the Bible tells us that 5,000 men were there, that's not counting the women and children.

Picture 1

In fact Jesus was so good at holding the people's attention that they stayed all day listening to him. As it got later into the afternoon the disciples said to Jesus, 'Look, it's getting late, these people need to go home, they must be getting hungry.'

Jesus then spoke to his disciples and said, 'They do not need to go away, you give them something to eat.' This put the disciples into a real panic, there were no shops on the hillside of Galilee and Philip (one of the disciples) had already worked out it would take eight months' wages to feed all these people – what were they going to do?

41

Picture 2   In the crowd that day there was a young boy who had not eaten his picnic, he had five small rolls and two fish. He went up to one of the disciples (a man called Andrew) and said that he was prepared to share his food. Andrew took the boy with his bread and fish to Jesus. Turning to the disciples, Jesus told them to sit the crowds down on the hillside in groups of fifties and one hundreds.

Picture 3   Jesus then took the bread and fish, he prayed thanking God for the food, and then broke it into pieces and told the disciples to give the food out to the people. They all took as much as they wanted. There was plenty to go around. Everyone had more than enough to eat and was satisfied. It was a miracle! After everyone had eaten, Jesus told the disciples to go round and collect all the scraps that were left over.

Picture 4   The disciples filled up twelve baskets of leftover fish and bread. It was truly amazing. One young boy had been prepared to share his picnic with Jesus and over 5,000 people left that hillside with full stomachs!

Application

We all appreciate it when someone shares something they have with us, but how good are we at sharing what we have with others?

- What do we have that we can share – perhaps with those in need?

- What are we prepared to share with others to help satisfy them?

The young boy in the story shared his lunch, but let's not necessarily think about giving our food away! Maybe we need to think about sharing our favourite toy with a friend!

Whoever we are, we all have something that we can share with others. Maybe you can share some of your time listening to someone who needs to talk. Perhaps you enjoy writing stories or poems, or maybe you can draw or paint lovely pictures, all these things can be shared for others to enjoy. Maybe your gift is playing a musical instrument or singing, thereby bringing pleasure to other people.

No matter who you are, you have something to offer. Are you prepared to share it today!

Suggested Songs

A boy gave to Jesus (*Junior Praise*, 1)

Who took fish and bread (*Junior Praise*, 286)

Make me a channel of your peace (*Junior Praise*, 161; *Kidsource*, 248)

The little boy (Tune – *Junior Praise*, 220) – see opposite.

Closing Thoughts/Prayer

Dear God,

thank you that we are all special and that we all have something that we can share with other people.

Please enable us to use whatever gifts and talents we have to help and bring enjoyment to others.

Amen.

Possible Classroom Follow-up

- Discuss
  - What things/abilities do the children have that they can share with others?
  - How can using these abilities help others in the school?

- Write a poem or song about the story. (If writing a song use a simple tune that you already know – example below.)

(Tune – *Junior Praise*, 220)

The little boy had a picnic lunch,
the little boy had a picnic lunch,
the little boy had a picnic lunch,
which he gave to Jesus.

Jesus said, 'Thank you for all the food', (x3)
gave it to his disciples.

Over 5,000 people then were fed (x3)
with lots of food left over.

Thank you, Lord, for all our food, (x3)
help us to share with others.

Picture 1

Picture 2

Picture 3

Picture 4

THE FOUR FRIENDS _____

Bible References   Matthew 9:2-8

Mark 2:2-12

Luke 5:18-26

Aim   To think about our friends and friendships and to question – am I a good friend to others?

Introduction   Either: a. Play or sing a song about friends, perhaps the theme song from *Friends* or 'We're your friends' (*Jungle Book*).

or

b. Talk about what friends are:

  – People whose company we enjoy

  – People who have similar interests to us

  – People who help us in difficult times

  – People who we share things with

  – People we care for other than our families

Bible Story   This is a true story that we read in the Bible, about a group of very good friends. It begins with . . .

Picture 1   . . . a certain man who was paralysed – this meant he could not move and walk around, he had to lie all day and night on a mattress. He couldn't work, the only way he could get money was by lying in the street begging. But he did have four very good friends. One day these four friends got to hear that Jesus was at a house in the town and knowing that he had healed lots of people, the four decided they would take their sick friend to see Jesus.

Picture 2   They carefully lifted up their sick friend on his mattress and carried him all the way to the house where Jesus was, but when they arrived they could see crowds of people were trying to get in to see Jesus – the house was already packed full. Not only were people crowded inside the house, there were people in the doorways, people peering in the windows, there was no room anywhere. It seemed hopeless, how were they going to get inside? However, instead of giving up, the four friends came up with a brilliant idea . . .

Picture 3 . . . they had seen the steps going up the outside of the house on to the flat roof, so they carried their friend up onto the roof and then started digging through the roof. Many houses in Bible times would have been made from mud and straw bricks which were then plastered over. We're not certain what this house was made from, but we do know that these friends made a large hole in the roof of this house and then very carefully they . . .

Picture 4 . . . lowered their friend down through the roof of the house. Jesus realised what lengths they had gone to in order to bring their friend to him. He knew they were good, reliable mates. Looking at the paralysed man Jesus told him to get up. Immediately he stood up, picked up his mattress and was able to walk home. He was completely healed.

Application

It was great that Jesus was able to make that man better, but he could only do that because the four friends had been prepared to work together as a team and put themselves out to help their mate. Imagine if, while carrying the sick man on his stretcher, the four friends had an argument and started pulling in different directions. Their friend would have fallen to the ground – they had to co-operate with each other.

On arriving at the house and not being able to get in they could have given up and gone home, but they put themselves out by carrying their sick friend onto the roof and making a hole to lower him through. The Bible doesn't tell us, but they sound like the kind of people who would have mended the roof afterwards!

- They were friends who were prepared to get involved in their friendship and put themselves out. Are your friends like that?
- If you want friends like that then surely you have to be that sort of friend yourself?
- Are you prepared to help your friends when they need it?
- Think how you can be a good friend today.

Suggested Songs

Shalom, my friend (*Junior Praise*, 217)

Thank you for my friends (*Tinderbox*, 31)

Shake a friend's hand (*Kidsource*, 293)

Closing Thoughts/Prayer

Dear God,

thank you for my friends,

please help me to think about how I can be a good friend to others and help me put those thoughts into action.

Amen.

Possible Classroom Follow-up

- Discuss
  - What qualities do you look for in a friend?
  - Is there such a thing as a bad friend?
- Write a poem about your special friends.

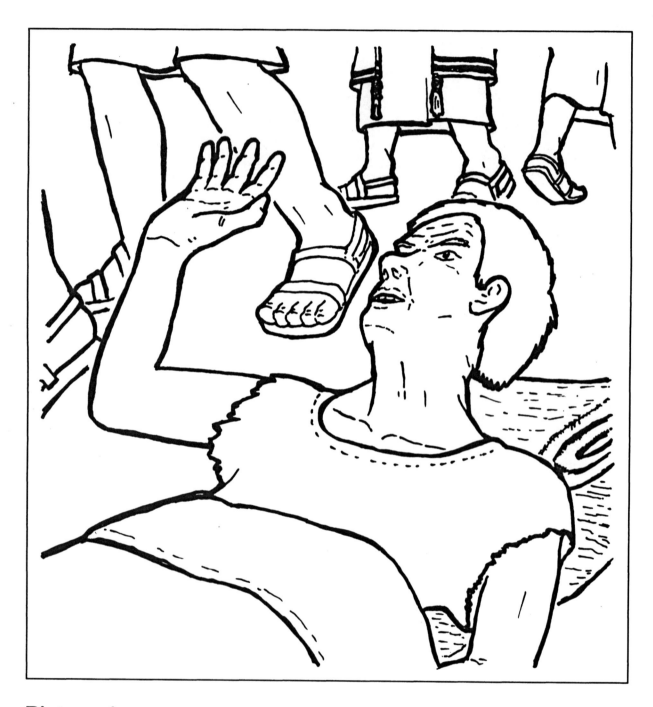

Picture 1

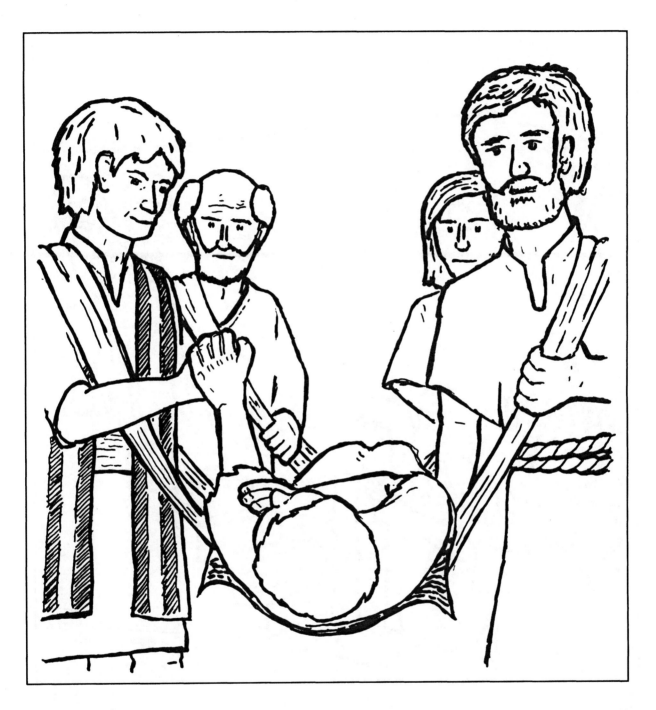

Picture 2

Picture 3

Picture 4

BLIND BARTIMAEUS _____

Bible References   Mark 10:46-52

Luke 18:35-42

Aim   To encourage the children to consider the type of people they are and have the potential to be.

Introduction   Either a. Talk about our five senses – touch/taste/hearing/smell/sight. In particular, how important is our sight?

or

b. Blindfold a volunteer and get them to guess the identity of three or four objects by using their other senses:

e.g. bottle of perfume (smell/touch)
    tambourine (touch/hearing)
    jar of jam (smell/taste/touch)
    a carrot (smell/taste/touch)

Bring out the point that with *sight* you would immediately know what the object was, but it's harder having to use the other senses. *(You could add to this by using objects that are all the same colour and bringing out the point that only the sense of* sight *can tell you colour.)*

Bible Story   This is a story about a man who couldn't see, not because he was blindfolded but because he was blind.

Picture 1   JERICHO: The story happened around 2,000 years ago in a city about 2,000 miles from here. A very famous city in Israel called Jericho. Jericho is an oasis (not the band) and it is also known as 'The City of Palms'.

Picture 2   JESUS: One day a very famous man – who you have probably heard a lot about – visited Jericho. His name was Jesus. He had said and done lots of amazing things and was usually followed around by . . .

Picture 3   CROWDS: . . . crowds of people. On this day Jericho was bursting with people. They hadn't come to watch Jericho Rovers play at home, they all wanted to see and hear Jesus. We don't know too much about the people in the crowd, but we do know a little about one man, his name was . . .

Picture 4   BARTIMAEUS: . . . Bart. No, not Bart Simpson, but BARTIMAEUS. And Bartimaeus was . . .

Picture 5   BLIND: . . . blind. He couldn't see anything! Sadly, in those days, if you were blind no one would give you a job and there were no social security benefits. Bartimaeus would have to sit by the side of the road with his arm outstretched, begging for money or food. But, today something was different. The noise made by the crowds was louder than usual, there was an excited buzz going around. Bartimaeus asked some passers-by 'What's happening, what's going on?'

'Jesus is in town,' they told him. 'You know, the man who has healed the sick and fed the hungry. He's here – today!' Bartimaeus began to feel very excited. This was his big moment. The chance he'd been waiting for.

So he started shouting at the top of his voice, 'Jesus, Jesus of Nazareth, over here, please help me!'

Picture 6   HINDERED: As he started to shout, some people in the crowd just walked by, completely ignoring him. Lots of others actually hindered him. They got very angry with him, 'Shut-up!' they shouted. 'We haven't come here to listen to a beggar like you. We want to hear Jesus, so be quiet!'

But Bartimaeus was desperate, he didn't give up. He kept on shouting, 'Jesus, over here, please help me!'

Picture 7   HELPED: Above the noise of the crowd, Jesus heard his cries for help. He stopped and said to a few people, 'Go and help that man and bring him to me.' Just a few people in the crowd did as Jesus asked. They went over to Bartimaeus, helped him to his feet and led him by the arm through the large crowd, to where Jesus was standing. He would never have made it on his own – remember he was blind, he would have tripped, stumbled, and apart from that, would not have known exactly where Jesus was. He needed help.

Picture 8   HEALED: In front of all the crowd, Jesus said to Bartimaeus, 'What do you want me to do for you?'

Bartimaeus simply replied, 'I want to be able to see.'

Jesus said to him, 'Because of your faith, you believe I can heal you and I will.' Immediately, Bartimaeus was able to see, words can't begin to describe how he felt, it was really fantastic, from that moment on his life was completely changed.

Application

• Who were the people who made a difference for Bartimaeus?

    – Was it the people who walked by, totally ignoring his cries for help?

No. Today we would say they 'turned a blind eye to him!'

(At this point you may want to reintroduce picture 5 – BLIND)

– Was it those cruel people who hindered him, by shouting abuse and demanding that he be quiet?

No. Today we would say they were 'blinded by their prejudice'.

• When you think about it, the people who really made a difference in Bartimaeus' life were . . .

  – The few people who helped him to his feet and led him through the crowd to meet Jesus, and Jesus of course, who healed him by restoring his sight.

  – What sort of people are you? Ignorers? Hinderers? Helpers? Healers?

• Maybe there are some children in this assembly hall today who in years to come will become carers, nurses, doctors, even famous brain or eye surgeons. Maybe the scientist who discovers a cure for cancer! There are so many different ways that we can be of help to others. The potential is enormous. The decision is yours. What sort of person do you want to be?

Suggested Songs

Shalom, my friend (*Junior Praise*, 217)

When I needed a neighbour (*Junior Praise*, 275)

Closing Thoughts/Prayer

Dear God,

thank you for all the people who look after, care for and help us.

Please help us to have the right attitude towards others, not ignoring or hindering those who are in need.

Show us how we can best help other people.

Amen.

Possible Classroom Follow-up

Discuss

• Why different people in the crowd reacted in the ways they did toward Bartimaeus.

• Ask the children to be honest and say what they think they would have done and why.

• How this incident relates to what goes on in the school playground.

Jericho

Jesus

Crowds

Bartimaeus

Blind

Hindered

Helped

Healed

THE PARABLE OF THE LOST SHEEP___

Bible References   Matthew 18:10-14

Luke 15:1-7

Aim
- To look at what is meant by a parable and how Jesus used visual illustrations to explain Biblical truths.
- To look at God's love through this parable.

Introduction   If you had lived in Israel at the time of Jesus you would have seen lots of different things that we don't often see in England today. For example, you would see farmers sowing seed in their fields by hand (not using tractors as we would). You would see shepherds roaming around the hills looking after the sheep, men fishing with nets on the sea, figs growing on the trees.

Jesus was an excellent teacher and he took many of these every-day situations and told stories about them. Lots of these stories that have become known as PARABLES *(show word)*, help us to understand how God cares for his people.

Parables can have an obvious and a hidden meaning, they can teach us something very important that we might otherwise find difficult to understand.

Quiz   The answers to the following questions are all 'hidden' in the word PARABLES.

See if you can find the answer to these questions – all the answers can be spelt out using the letters P - A - R - A - B - L - E - S.

1. These swingers love bananas.   APES

2. These 'Teddies' are undressed.   BARE

3. These gentlemen are all titled.   EARLS

4. Frogs do this when they take-off.   LEAP

5. This person has obviously not got a suntan.   PALE

6. Not fantasy or fiction but ____ .   REAL

7. You could get a good bargain here.   SALE

8. Different types of beer.   ALES

9. Bundles of hay or straw.   BALES

10. The ones on the corn are always deaf.   EARS

11. Look very closely at a Shakespearean King.   LEAR

12. Maybe this fruit grows in twos.   PEARS

13. A modern style of very rhythmic music.   RAP

14. The liquid produced by a plant or tree.   SAP

15. A type of sword and a type of tiger.   SABRE

Bible Story

(This story has been written for audience participation – as the appropriate number is shown the children are encouraged to call it out.)

Probably **1** of the most famous parables that Jesus told was about a shepherd and his sheep. The shepherd had **100** sheep. He loved and cared for all **100** of them. Everyday he would let them out **2** graze in the fields and at night he would round them up and count them, **2** make sure that every **1** of them had come back safely. He would start **1, 2** and count right up to **99, 100.** The shepherd cared **4** all his sheep, so **1** night when he started counting **1, 2,** and only reached **99,** he started to get worried . . . was **1** of his sheep missing?

He counted again **1, 2** and so on until **99,** yes, he had counted right. **1** of the sheep was missing! The shepherd knew he had to find his **1** lost sheep. He put the **99** safely into a field and set off to look for him. The shepherd was really worried, where was his **1** missing sheep? He walked across the fields thinking to himself . . .

. . . Was his sheep sick? – maybe it was something he **8.**

. . . What if he'd got lost! – it was a long way **4** a sheep to roam.

. . . Perhaps he was in danger! – and needed some **1** to help him.

The shepherd kept searching, determined to find his sheep, even though it got very late. Maybe even after **8.** He walked and walked, and then . . . in the distance he saw him. The shepherd ran **2** wards his sheep, gathered him up in his arms and carried him back **2** the farm. The **1** sheep was now safely reunited with the other **99.** The shepherd was really happy, he was no longer **1** sheep short! He called all his friends and neighbours in **2** celebrate with a party. They **8** and drank, rejoicing with the shepherd. He was so delighted that all **100** of his sheep were safe.

Application

Can you remember how many meanings parables have? (Two)

- The obvious meaning is quite easy to understand – it's just a good story about a shepherd, who on discovering one of his sheep was missing went and looked for it, not giving up until he found it.

- The hidden meaning in this parable is that God is like the shepherd and we are like the sheep. We may ignore God, we may think we are running away from him, but that still doesn't stop him from loving and caring for us.

Suggested Songs

I am a sheep (*Junior Praise 2*, 373)

The Lord's my shepherd (*Junior Praise*, 243)

The Lord is my shepherd (*Junior Praise*, 244)

Closing Thoughts/Prayer

Dear God,

thank you for the Bible and that we can learn so much from the parables Jesus told.

Please help us to learn to love and care for each other in the same way you love and care for us.

Amen.

Possible Classroom Follow-up

- Read Psalm 23 from the Bible and list some of the ways in which the Lord helps the author of this psalm (King David).

For example . . .

v.1 Provides all he needs.

v.2 Provides rest and leads him.

v.3 Gives new strength and helps him.

v.4 Takes away fear, guards, guides and comforts.

v.5 Provides food for him.

v.6 Will always be with him

- Write your own modern-day parable.

PARABLES

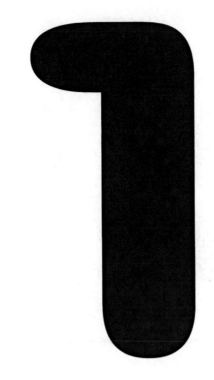

THE PARABLE OF
THE GOOD SAMARITAN _____

Bible Reference   Luke 10:25-37

Aim   To think about who is my neighbour and how I can be a good neighbour to others.

Introduction   Either: a. Play/sing the theme tune from the *Neighbours* TV programme.

or

b. Talk in general terms about your neighbours and how you relate to them.

Bible Story   In the Bible you can read a lot about neighbours and how we should love them and care for them. One day a man went up to Jesus and asked him the question: 'Who is my neighbour?' Jesus answered the man by telling him a story:

Picture 1   A man from Jerusalem had to go on a long journey to another city called Jericho, so he packed up some clothes and food, loaded up his donkey and set off on his journey. Travelling to Jericho was not easy as it meant going over some very barren, rocky hills.

Picture 2   It was a great hiding place for thieves and robbers. From behind the rocks they could see people travelling along the road. They could tell if they were alone and if they had anything worth stealing. Unfortunately the traveller from Jerusalem was seen and before long . . .

Picture 3   . . . the thieves and robbers ran out from behind the rocks and attacked the man. They beat him up and stole everything he had – money, food, clothes and even his donkey.

Picture 4   They ran off leaving the man lying badly injured on the road. He couldn't move, he was in great pain, he thought he was going to die. Then he heard footsteps . . . someone was coming along the road towards him.

Picture 5   It was a priest, a very important person. The traveller thought to himself, 'This man is bound to stop and help!' But the priest was very busy and didn't want to get involved and so, even though he saw how badly the man was injured, he crossed over to the far side of the road and quickly walked by, ignoring the cries for help. The poor man lay there. Then a little later he heard some more footsteps, someone else was coming along the road. It was . . .

Picture 6   . . . a Levite, another very important person. Surely he would stop and help! However, the Levite was busy and didn't want to get involved, besides, those robbers might come back! Like the priest, he too crossed over to the other side of the road and hurried on by. The injured man was desperate. Was no one prepared to help him? Just then he heard someone else coming down the road. He looked up hopefully, but when he saw who was coming all his hopes were dashed, of all the people it could have been it was . . .

Picture 7   . . . a Samaritan! This man was not a Jew like the traveller from Jerusalem. Very sadly, Jews and Samaritans had been bitter enemies for years and normally would not even speak to each other. However, the traveller was in for a real surprise, because the Samaritan came straight over to him and began to bandage up his wounds. Then this very kind Samaritan lifted the injured man on to his donkey and . . .

Picture 8   . . . the two men continued their journey along the road together until they came to a hotel. The Samaritan carried the wounded man into the hotel, booked him into a room and continued to care for him. The following day before resuming his journey, the Samaritan gave the hotel-manager some money and asked him to look after the Jew until he was better. 'If it costs more than this,' the Samaritan said, 'then I'll pay the rest next time I'm passing by.'

The question Jesus asked after telling this story was – 'Which one of the three was a really good neighbour?'
(Hopefully the children will be eager to answer this question.)

Application

Jesus was trying to teach that everyone is our neighbour, not just the people who live next door. Not just our friends, not just the people we like, but everyone that we meet.

• How do you treat your neighbours?

• Do you ignore them like the priest and Levite or are you like the good Samaritan, prepared to help when problems and difficulties arise?

(At this point you may want to relate a personal account of how someone has been a good neighbour to you or ask the children to think how they could be good neighbours in school or at home.)

Spend a few moments thinking how you can be a really good neighbour to someone today.

Suggested Songs

When I needed a neighbour (*Junior Praise*, 275)

Would you walk by on the other side (*Come and Praise*, 70)

Closing Thoughts/Prayer

Dear God,

thank you for all the people who look after and take care of us and in doing so demonstrate they are good neighbours.

Please help us to be good neighbours and to think about how we can help and care for others.

Amen.

Possible Classroom Follow-up

• Discuss as a class what a good neighbour would and would not do.

• Imagine the Good Samaritan's friends found out what he had done.

 – How do you think they would have reacted knowing he helped a Jew?

• Think about what you would have done in this situation.

Picture 1

Picture 2

Picture 3

Picture 4

Picture 5

Picture 6

Picture 7

Picture 8

THE PARABLE OF THE UNFORGIVING SERVANT

Bible Reference   Matthew 18:23-35

Aim   To think about anger and forgiveness and being prepared to forgive others.

Introduction   Human beings are able to express how they are feeling through what we call emotions. We can often tell what people are feeling just by looking at what is known as their body language. *(Either by using the whole school or a couple of dramatic volunteers, introduce emotions and body language.)*

How do you look when you are: HAPPY
SAD
EMBARRASSED
SCARED
SURPRISED
THOUGHTFUL
ANGRY

Some of these strong emotions come out in the story. See if you can spot them.

Bible Story   One day Peter (one of the disciples) asked Jesus how many times he should forgive someone. Jesus responded my telling him a parable about a servant who worked for a King.

Picture 1   This servant had a very important position in the palace, he and others in this position were allowed to borrow money from the King. Sometimes to invest it to try and make more money, other times they would borrow money to buy things they wanted for themselves and their families. Now the day had come for this servant to pay back to the King all the money he owed. When the King told him that the total he had borrowed amounted to millions of pounds the servant knew he was in big trouble!

Picture 2   He had not got millions of pounds to pay the King back. So the King demanded that the servant should lose his job, all his possessions be sold and that his wife and children would become the King's slaves. The servant pleaded with the King, 'Be patient with me and I will pay back everything,' but deep down the servant knew he could never pay back the whole amount.

Now the King was a very generous man, he knew his servant couldn't pay him back and he took pity on him so he said to his servant, 'I'll forgive you the whole amount – you don't have to pay me anything back.'

Picture 3   The servant was delighted, he'd been forgiven millions of pounds worth of debt, he had been let off, his home and family were safe – it was great. He went off happily around the palace until . . . he met another servant and a thought struck him . . .

Picture 4   . . . this guy owes me some money, so he said to him, 'Hey, you owe me £2.00 – I want it back now!' The second servant didn't know what to do, he hadn't got £2.00 so he begged for time to get the money and pay it back.

Picture 5   But the servant didn't listen, instead he got very angry, shouting at the poor man, he demanded his money straight away or else he would send him to prison.

Picture 6   The poor man couldn't pay straight away and so the first servant had him imprisoned. When other people in the palace heard what had happened they were really annoyed so they went and told the King.

Picture 7   The King was very upset and really angry, he summoned the servant in to see him. 'I let you off repaying me millions of pounds because you begged me to,' he said to the servant 'and yet you couldn't forgive someone who owed you just £2.00.' The servant had no excuse for his behaviour and the King had him sent to . . .

Picture 8   . . . prison, until he paid back all the millions of pounds he owed.

Application   Sometimes in life we can make some really big mistakes. It's easy to say or do something that can really hurt or upset someone. Very often that person can be a friend. However it's great when that person is prepared to forgive us.

- However are we always as forgiving of other people?

- Sometimes we can lose our temper over the smallest thing and find it very difficult to forgive. Doctors will tell you that holding onto anger and bitterness can make us physically ill.

- The Bible has much to say on this subject, perhaps it could be all summed up in the words of Jesus when he said, 'In everything, do to others what you would have them do to you.' (Matthew 7:12, NIV)

Suggested Songs

Make me a channel (*Junior Praise*, 161; *Kidsource*, 248)

Shalom, my friend (*Junior Praise*, 217)

Closing Thoughts/Prayer

Dear God,

thank you that when we've made mistakes in the past people have been prepared to forgive us.

When we make mistakes in the future, help us to quickly recognise them for what they are and be honest and sincere in asking for forgiveness.

Also really help us to have the ability to forgive others when they say and do things that hurt or upset us.

Amen.

Possible Classroom Follow-up

- Ask the children if they think it is easier to get angry with friends and family or people they don't know so well. Why?

- If it is near Easter you may consider asking the children to think about what Jesus prayed as he was crucified . . . 'Father forgive them, for they do not know what they are doing.' (Luke 23:34)

Picture 1

Picture 2

Picture 3

Picture 4

Picture 5

Picture 6

Picture 7

Picture 8

THE PARABLE OF THE WISE AND FOOLISH MEN _____

Bible References Matthew 7:24-27

Luke 6:47-49

Aim To think about good advice and how following it can help us.

Introduction Either: a. Share from your own experience a time when you did or didn't take the good advice you were given and the subsequent result.

or

b. Ask the children to think about what is good advice and feed-back why it is important to follow it, what are the consequences of not listening to good advice, for example:

– School Rules (Do not run down the corridor)

– Signs (Wet Paint/Keep Off The Grass)

– Warnings (Hot – Do Not Touch/Danger)

Bible Story

Picture 1 Jesus told of two men who both wanted to build houses. The first man was a wise man, he had learnt about building houses and how they needed a firm foundation. It would mean a lot of hard work, but the wise man followed the good advice he had learnt, fetched his spade and started to dig deep into the ground.

Picture 2 After he had dug down really deep he began to build with bricks on a foundation of solid rock. He carefully cemented the bricks together, making sure they were all firmly in place. It was a long job but the wise man kept on working slowly and carefully, gradually building his house.

Picture 3 Meanwhile, the other man had started work on his house. But he really was a foolish man because he thought he knew best and ignored all the advice he had been given on building houses. He couldn't be bothered to dig foundations, that was too much like hard work! He just got the bricks, slopped on cement and piled them on top of each other. He didn't even try to keep them straight or level!

Picture 4   The foolish man kept building until his house was finished. He was delighted with it and it hadn't taken too long to build. 'I'm sure I'm going to be very happy in my new house', he said to himself.

Picture 5   Finally the wise man finished building his house. It had taken a lot of time and effort, but he was really pleased with his new home. It was solidly built on a firm foundation. Both men then moved into their new houses and everything was OK for a while, but . . .

Picture 6   . . . a storm blew up! The sky grew dark, lightning flashed, the thunder roared, the rain poured down. It was so heavy that the ground could not absorb all the water and the puddles grew larger and larger. Slowly the water started to rise and as the floods spread and more rain came down, the foolish man realised that the water was washing away the soil on which his house was built.

Picture 7   The storm raged, the water level continued to rise and because the foolish man's house had no foundation, suddenly the whole building collapsed around his ears!

Picture 8   Meanwhile, the wise man, who had built on a good solid foundation, was safe and dry in his house, secure from the storm.

Application

Jesus was telling that story to people nearly 2,000 years ago, even then people knew that houses needed a foundation and builders today know that you need to have plans and a firm foundation before building anything. So what was Jesus getting at?

Jesus was relating the two houses to people's lives and explaining how they need to build their lives on a firm foundation. There are many things, like money and material possessions that people try to build their lives on, but these can let them down badly.

Listening to and taking the good advice we are given is not always seen as the 'cool' thing to do. However it is very important to do so. Sometimes we ignore good advice, we may even act upon bad advice and everything may seem OK for a little while, but when life gets tough and difficult situations develop (like the storm in the story) are we able to stand or do we crumble under the pressure?

The Bible tells us that Jesus is the solid rock on which we need to build our lives.

Suggested Songs

The wise man built his house upon the rock (*Junior Praise*, 252; *Kidsource*, 366)

Don't build your house on the sandy land (*Junior Praise*, 39; *Kidsource*, 40)

Closing Thoughts/Prayer

Dear God,

help us not to be like the foolish man in the story who couldn't be bothered to follow the good advice and suffered as a result.

Instead, help us to be like the wise man, who not only listened to the good advice but acted upon it.

Please help us build our lives on a solid foundation.

Amen.

Possible Classroom Follow-up

- Discuss as a class what is 'good' and what is 'bad' advice.
- Explore in more detail the consequences of the actions we take.
- Introduce and discuss the concept of responsibility for our actions.

Picture 1

Picture 2

Picture 3

Picture 4

Picture 5

Picture 6

Picture 7

Picture 8

TAKE CARE _____

This assembly is designed with Key Stage 1 children in mind. However, it could well be used as a class assembly for Key Stage 2, with a group of children taking each theme and presenting their own thoughts and pictures on how to take care.

Aim

To think about all the wonderful things we have and how we should take care of them.

Introduction

TAKE CARE – these are two words that we hear many times, you may hear people say to you:

'TAKE CARE as you cross the road'

'You must TAKE more CARE with your writing'

'TAKE CARE you don't drop that'

Taking care of ourselves and things around us is important. Let's look at what we need to TAKE CARE of:

Story

(The idea is to interact with your audience – encouraging feedback from the questions.)

Teeth

– Who cleaned their teeth this morning?

– What do you need to clean your teeth properly?

– If you have problems with your teeth, who can you visit?

– What will happen if you do not clean them?

Having good, strong, healthy teeth is important. We need to TAKE CARE of them.

Animals

– Who has a pet at home?

– Who has a cat? dog? rabbit? fish? hamster? unusual pet?

– If your pet lives in a cage, what do you need to do to care for it?

– What do you need to do to care for your cat/dog?

– Who has helped the wildlife by putting food out for them?

– What type of animals have you helped?

Our pets can make us very happy, looking out and seeing the wildlife can be fascinating, but they will not survive unless we TAKE CARE of them.

Work   – Who has already worked hard this morning?

– Who finds doing their writing easy? spellings? sums?

– Why is it important that we learn to read and write?

When you get older and find a job, it's going to be very important that you do your work properly. At school you learn how to work well and do your best, so that later on in life you will know how to TAKE CARE over your work.

Bodies   – Who loves chips? ice cream? pizza? chocolate?

– What would happen to us if we only ate those foods?

– To keep our bodies fit and healthy, what should we eat?

– What else can we do to keep us fit and healthy?

Exercise, eating the right food, plenty of sleep, is important to keep us healthy. We need to TAKE CARE of our bodies.

Clothes   – Who goes home from school and changes into different clothes?

– What different clothes do we wear when playing football? ballet? swimming?

– What do we need to do when our clothes get dirty?

– What is in our clothes that tells us how to wash and care for them?

In some parts of the world, people are so poor they cannot afford to buy clothes and many live in rags or our second-hand clothes. We are fortunate in this country to have a choice of clothes to wear, but they are expensive, so it's important that we TAKE CARE of our clothes.

Family   – How many of you have got brothers? sisters?

– Who lives with their family in a flat? house? bungalow? boat?

– How can we show we care for our family?

Our families are very special and important to us. However, sometimes they may be the very people that we argue with the most! (Who argues with their brother or sister?). It may be tough at times, but it's good to try hard to TAKE CARE of our families.

Earth   – What is the name of the planet that we live on?

– In what ways do people spoil our planet?

– Can you think of things we can do to stop that happening?

– What action can you take to stop litter spoiling our school grounds?

We only have the one planet to live on and so it's very important that we learn to TAKE CARE of it.

Friends

— Who travels to school with a friend?

— Who has a friend in their class?

— What are some of the things you like to do with your friends?

— How can you show your friends that you care for them?

Like our families, our friends are very special people and if we learn to TAKE CARE of them they can be our friends for a long, long time.

Application

We have mentioned eight things we should TAKE CARE of. Perhaps you can think of more.

• Although taking care means we have to put in that extra bit of effort, it will certainly make our lives and the lives of others much better and happier.

Suggested Songs

Autumn days (*Come and Praise*, 4)

Have you seen the pussycat? (*Junior Praise*, 72; *Kidsource*, 100)

Thank you, Lord (*Junior Praise*, 232)

Closing Thoughts/Prayer

Dear God,

thank you for this lovely world and everything in it.

Thank you for all the people who care for us and help us.

Please help us to do our part by caring for our world and others around us.

Amen.

Possible Classroom Follow-up

• Discuss: how should we take care with . . . (classmates/playtimes/ school equipment/etc.)

• Write a project on one of the items mentioned in assembly, e.g. bodies – look at parts of the body, diet, health, exercise . . .

TEETH

ANIMALS

WORK

BODIES

CLOTHES

FAMILY

EARTH

FRIENDS

Lightning Source UK Ltd.
Milton Keynes UK
06 November 2010

162497UK00001B/6/P